What others have said about *Seven Choices:*

"Readers will welcome Elizabeth Neeld's guide to mourning and recovery...[the book] offers sound advice on how to adjust to change and form new life patterns and huma·   's."
Publisher's Weekly

"A gifted writer...Elizabeth Neel·   ·uel Johnson's first criterion for ger·   ·a-tionship between apparen·'   ·...· Compelling substance."
The W

"A highly original and me   ·n to the grieving process."
Psychology Toa   ·· *News*

"A useful, wide-ranging work...trenchant...pertinent..."
Kirkus Reviews

"*Seven Choices* is a profound book in many ways because the author really cares about people; her subtle suggestions bear the mark of someone who has been there...Deeply compassionate and very wise. This is a fine, sensitive book written by a very intelligent person. Extremely well done."
The Coast Book Review Service, Fullerton, CA

"My son was killed on a motorcycle eleven years ago, and, yes, there has been tremendous healing. *Seven Choices* is still very helpful to me, however, after all this time. Thank you."
SM, Maryland, letter to author

"I have read approximately thirty-five books on grief since my husband died last September, and for me, *Seven Choices*, is the one that helped me the most."
C. Lahr, writing to *Bereavement Magazine*

"Our support group has used *Seven Choices* several times for intensive, small-group series. Your wisdom, honesty and shared experience have equipped us with the necessary tools to move forward—as an informed choice!"
Pam Walker, Co-Founder, Young Widows' Support Group, Dayton, OH

Elizabeth Harper Neeld's eighteen
publications include:

*Seven Choices: Finding Daylight After Loss
Shatters Your World (Full Text)*

Sister Bernadette: Cowboy Nun from Texas

*A Sacred Primer: The Essential Guide
to Quiet Time and Prayer*

Yes! You Can Write

From the Plow to the Pulpit

Seven Choices Audio Book

The Challenge of Grief Video

Seven Choices

Choices

A POCKET GUIDE

*Finding Daylight After
Loss Shatters Your World*

ELIZABETH HARPER NEELD, PH.D.

www.elizabethharperneeld.com

Centerpoint Press
www.centerpointpress.com

The complete book, *Seven Choices: Finding Daylight After Loss Shatters Your World* (Reprint Edition ISBN 0446690503), is available at your local bookstore or on bookseller sites online.

Seven Choices: A Pocket Guide (ISBN 0937897442) is available from Centerpoint Press www.centerpointpress.com

The stories told in *Seven Choices* are true. In order to honor the privacy of the more than sixty generous individuals who discussed with me their grieving process, I have altered names and other features of the accounts.

CONTENTS

PROLOGUE

When we are experiencing a devastating loss, it hardly seems that there could be anything hopeful associated with such an unbalancing, painful experience. Yet, as Dr. George Pollock tells us, there is a process of active grieving—an "adaptive-transformational" process which he also calls a "change-creative gain" process—that is natural to human beings. This active grieving process, which begins when we perceive the first hints of loss, can result—if we make the right choices—in our finding a way to integrate the loss into our lives and to gain freedom from the domination of our grief.

Movement through this active grieving process is not a function of the passage of time. Rather, it is our choices that determine whether or not we reach Integration or Daylight. For at critical junctures in the process, we do make particular choices that move us forward toward constructive, creative outcomes or move us backward toward debilitating, destructive outcomes. You will find in the pages that follow (1) stories—my own story of the death of my young husband and stories from individuals who made constructive choices that resulted in their being able to love life again (2) identification of the different clusters of experiences that are normal when anyone is dealing with a loss and (3) identification of the proactive choice in each cluster of experiences that, if made, leads to integration and to the achievement of a "new normal" balance in our lives.

A map of the terrain of this active grieving process is on the opposite page. Remember this, however: A map never tells us how to travel. A map does not determine that everyone travels the same route, moves at the same speed, shares a set itinerary. A map does not dictate, prescribe, or even describe an individual's movement. A map does, however, name. A map can help us find where we are when we think we are lost. A map shows possibilities and provides ideas for where else there is for us to go. At all times, however, every individual is the person holding the map.

We do not, of course—even when we make the right choices—move along this terrain of the active grieving process in a lock-step, predictable manner. We make progress, regress, skip clusters of experiences, redo some phases many times—all depending on our own way of grieving. There is no right way to grieve; there is no direct path.

You can use the chapters that follow as a personal guidebook to help you make your way through the unfamiliar, upsetting, life-threatening experience of loss. By making productive choices along the way, you will reach creative outcomes where you will find your grief lightened. New energies will be available to you: *a quickened verve for living, new connections, a creative product, the ability to feel peaceful or happy or well again, the desire to get back to work or to do things you enjoyed doing in the past, a sense of release, a new calm.*

To learn as much as we can, then, about this active grieving process is one of the most valuable things we can do for ourselves when we have experienced a loss. Not only will you learn in the pages that follow what is normal when you deal with a loss; but, much more importantly, you will become aware of the critical role each of us plays in how our personal loss becomes integrated into the whole of our lives.

To remember: *A map never tells us how to travel. A map does not determine that everyone travels the same route, moves at the same speed, shares a set itinerary. A map does not dictate, prescribe, or even describe an individual's movement. A map does, however, name. A map can help us find where we are when we think we are lost. A map shows possibilities and provides ideas for where else there is for us to go. At all times, however, every individual is the person holding the map.*

3

IMPACT:

Experiencing the Unthinkable

W ork had gone well today, and after supper Greg had said, "Want to join me for a six-mile run?"

"No, sir, offer declined," I said. "I'll do the two-mile route and see you back here when you're finished."

So I had run to the Possum Creek bridge and back, and it was now time—past time—for Greg to be home. Minutes passed. "I bet these hills *did* get to him," I said to myself. "He's probably walking the last miles. I'll take the car and go pick him up; he'll appreciate a ride back home."

I started the car and guided it carefully over the big roots of the trees that grew all the way up to the edge of the cabin. I turned onto the paved road from the cabin lane. It was that time between daylight and dark that makes one feel lonesome and melancholy. Reaching the bridge at Possum Creek, I noticed how still and deep the water looked. Everything was covered with that kind of gray-green light left in the mountains when the sun had almost gone down. I crossed the bridge and rounded a curve.

There I came upon a scene of confusion. Large groups of people were standing on both sides of the road and spilling out into it. Carefully, I treaded my way through the crowd. I drove past the black-and-white car that belonged to the sheriff's patrol. I drove past the orange-and-white ambulance parked in the gravel on the left-hand side of the road. What held my attention was getting back onto the open road.

The trees and bushes were thick and grew close to the pavement. "It'll be easy to miss him if you're not careful," I reminded myself as I left the crowd behind. So I drove slowly, looking carefully to the right and to the left.

There he is! I see him! It was a glimpse of Greg's orange running shorts. I had known I would find him taking it slow and easy up and down these hills! I accelerated the car and exhaled a sigh of relief. How long, I wondered, had I been holding my breath?

But when I got to the spot where Greg was, the orange was a cylinder that had been mounted on a post, meant to hold a newspaper.

By now I had reached the country store that I knew was Greg's three-mile turnaround point. "I've just missed him somewhere on the road," I said, speaking aloud to no one but myself. "I'll turn around here. I know I'll see him on the way back. I've just managed to miss him."

When I got to the curve above Possum Creek, the large crowd was still there. So was the black-and-white car that belonged to the sheriff's patrol. And so was the orange-and-white ambulance.

I noticed a man standing in the middle of the road. He seemed to be directing traffic.

"What happened?" I asked, rolling down the window when I got abreast of him.

"Lady, move on. You're blocking traffic," was the man's reply.

I eased the car on down toward another man who was also standing in the middle of the road. This man appeared to be in charge.

"Sir, what happened?" I asked.

"We found a man in the ditch," he answered.

"Well, I'm looking for my husband," I said. "My husband went for a six-mile run, and he hasn't come home yet."

For a few seconds the man said nothing. Then he spoke in a voice so low that I could hardly hear him. "Ma'am, I think you should pull your car over to the side of the road." I felt no emotion. I asked no additional questions. If there was any connection between what was happening beside that road and my life, it still was not apparent to me. But I did what I was told. I pulled over to the side of the road.

There was a place I could park on the gravel. I pulled in beyond the ambulance and turned off the motor. By the time I put my feet on the ground outside the car, that man and another were there by my open door. They were waiting for me to get out of the car.

From my seat, I looked up at the two strange men. It was only then that I realized that the man they had found in the ditch and the man I was looking for were probably one and the same.

"Is he dead,' I asked.

There was a long silence. One of the men finally answered.

"Yes, ma'am. He is."

I got out of the car. One man stood on my right side and one on my left. We began to walk, not touching, toward the ambulance. Greg, my husband, was dead.

IMPACT: Experiencing the Unthinkable

What is normal?
- Presence of strong emotion
- Absence of emotion and feeling
- Need to roam; inability to sit still
- Inability to concentrate

- Yearning and longing
- Being dominated by memories
- Body biorhythms disturbed (sleep, eating, etc.)
- Feeling numb
- Plagued by anger, guilt, blame
- Experiencing fear, confusion, disorientation
- Having no hope

These IMPACT reactions are universal, and they are automatic. The responses are elemental, ancient, connected to human beings' need for balance and order in our lives and to our desire for remaining bonded and connected to those around us.

Here are stories from people who generously told me their stories of what it was like for them during IMPACT:

Seeing the Lost One
A young widow speaks:

I walked past the stairs, and out of the corner of my eye, I saw him sitting on the top step. He was putting his tennis shoes on. The image was so vivid. He was bent over tying his shoe just the way he always did, with his racket up against his knee. The scene startled me so much that I jerked to a stop. But when I looked again, the step was bare.

Confusion and Disorientation
A grieving partner told this story:

I cannot remember my own phone number. I took the wrong turn coming home from work today, and we've lived in the same place for four years. My mind just will not work. I start from one place to another in the office and forget where I was headed or why. I cannot make sense of reports, the same kind of reports that I have been receiving from my colleagues since I went to work at this company. Our boss asked us in a staff meeting one day this week to consider a particular business situation from a completely different point of view than we would ordinarily have done. In the past I've always enjoyed this kind of challenge to think "outside the box." But for the life of me, I could see only the obvious. I was unable to imagine a single alternative.

The CHOICE for
IMPACT: Experiencing the Unthinkable

We can choose to experience and express our grief fully.

You might wonder: if the responses during this time are automatic, how could an individual *not* make the choice to experience and express grief fully?

That's the paradox. The automatic, natural responses occur, but *we* decide whether to experience fully these responses or to try to stifle and suppress them.

And there are many reasons we might choose to suppress our grief instead of express it. The pain might seem unbearable. It may seem more reasonable, since nothing can be done about the loss, to try to forget it—to put it behind us—as quickly as possible. People around us may encourage us "to be brave," "to be strong," "to pull ourselves together." Or we may feel that if we don't rise above the loss, we are denying tenets of faith we have affirmed and lived by. Perhaps people around us may indicate—and we ourselves may believe—that sufficient time has passed for us to be finished with this particular cluster of responses to our loss. We may be embarrassed to express our grief in front of others. We may fear we are going crazy because we think strange thoughts and do weird things. Perhaps we decide to curtail the expression of our grief because it is interfering with our daily activities.

But it is dangerous not to choose to express grief fully. Objective studies show that those who suppress their emotions have more physical and psychological ailments during the first month, remain disturbed much longer, and, even as long as thirteen months after the loss, are still displaying more marked disturbances than people who were willing to express fully their feelings following the loss.

What helps while I am expressing my grief fully during IMPACT:

- Stay close to people who love you.
- Talk to the lost person as if she or he were actually present.
- Ask for anything you need.
- Spend as much time as you can with someone who encourages you to grieve in any way you want to.
- Take care of yourself.
- Talk to a professional. There are wonderful counselors, pastoral care professionals, social workers, and therapists who can be a guide in this painful grieving process.

THE SECOND CRISIS:

Stumbling in the Dark

For weeks after I returned to Texas I lived a vagabond existence. I was afraid to stay in my house alone—the same professional woman who had lived by herself for three years in New York City, relishing every minute of the experience?

"This is *my* house," I finally said to myself angrily, "and I am going to live in it!" So I mustered up the courage to spend a night alone.

I timed my return from school in order to arrive as late as possible but still before darkness fell. I turned on the television as soon as I entered; at least I could hear voices. Then I went through the house, looking under every bed, in the bathtub, in every closet. When it started to get dark, I put a towel over the kitchen window.

I spent the evening sitting down and getting up. I made lists of things to do and then decided not to do them. I skipped supper and instead ate a quart of vanilla ice cream. At bedtime I moved from the upstairs to the downstairs bedroom in case I needed to get out of the house quickly to escape some intruder. I was afraid to undress, so I slept in my clothes. I put a pistol from Greg's college ROTC days by the bed, even though I did not know how to use it. I was still awake when the alarm went off in the morning.

So much of every day was taken up with unfamiliar and painful business. The legal and business affairs related to Greg's death seemed unending. Entering the lawyer's office, I would reassure myself, "No need to be concerned; this will be no problem. It's just a piece of legal business." I felt strong and capable. But when I started to tell the man why I was there, I discovered I was crying.

I worried constantly about not having enough money. At night I dreamed of dying a shriveled-up old woman in the poorhouse—a scene that always looked like something from a Dickens novel. When I got my first paycheck for the new school year, I realized that the monthly bills amounted to more than my salary. With Greg alive and both of us working, our financial future had been comfortable and secure. Now it was bleak and frightening.

Such were the concerns of my daily life. Nothing was the same. Everything was unfamiliar.

My place in the world was also drastically altered. People who had been friendly in the past were now awkward around me. The first time I went into the mailroom at the university, some of my colleagues were gathered around, passing the time and chatting. I walked in, and everything changed. The easy conversation turned to silence. The joviality turned to haste to get out of the room. Within seconds everyone was gone. Several people said hello to me as they passed; but no one mentioned Greg, even though some of them had written me notes when he died. One day an acquaintance came to the house to visit and stayed two hours. Not once was anything said that indicated that my husband had died, even though the woman had earlier sent me a lovely note of condolence. I understood this reluctance to talk of death, this awkwardness and avoidance; but I also hated it.

THE SECOND CRISIS: Stumbling in the Dark

What is normal?
- Daily life feeling disorganized and in disarray
- Loss of our "assumptive world;" recognition that the future we assumed we would have will never happen now
- Feelings of emptiness, helplessness, and hopelessness
- Sadness, depression, despondency and despair
- Decline in health; increase in accidents
- Questioning of long-held beliefs and philosophies
- Feeling of being suspended in mid-air, having no foundation
- Continued obsession with anger, guilt, and blame
- Being able to find no structure or shape for our lives
- Loneliness

The responses of THE SECOND CRISIS may be delayed reactions, occurring weeks, months, or even years after the loss. If anything, this time of Stumbling in the Dark feels worse than the original crisis–, the news of the loss itself. By this time you are discovering how totally your life has been changed by the loss. As time passes, you see even more new ways that your life has been affected. You come to see that this loss cannot be compensated for. It is irreversible. When all this becomes inescapably known, you experience the normal reactions of THE SECOND CRISIS.

Listen to these stories:

Feelings of Despair

A man remembers:

I decided that I would finally unpack and settle into this new place. The first thing I took out of the box was a Mr.

Coffee. Well, as I unloaded the coffeemaker, the glass decanter fell out and broke on the tile floor. I was so heart-broken that I just sat down, broken glass and all, and I cried. Like a little baby. I lost control.

I'd cut my finger on the glass, and some combination of things—the broken glass, me sitting there on the floor, completely worn out with dealing with all this, completely spent, the blood on my hands, the boxes around me, nothing, no good smells, no food cooking, no anything—made me feel total despair. "This is the beginning of death-in-life," I said to myself.

For at least a month I shook a lot; my voice trembled. I cried easily; I was angry and short with people without notice. I began behaving erratically—I'm not a drinker, but I'd buy a bottle of wine and drink the whole bottle in one night. I started cooking enormous meals, which I then couldn't eat because I didn't want them. In fact, I'd go without eating for days, just living on orange juice, coffee, candy. I lived a life of nobody-ness. It was a time of being helpless and hopeless.

A Loss of Faith

A mother speaks:

You know, when a child dies, in addition to the sense of loss, there is a sense of outrage because it's unnatural. It's not in the scheme of things. A parent should go first. There's also the sense of a wasted life. So many years to live. So much to live for. Now as a parent you can never know what the child might have become.

We have not been able to make the loss of our daughter compatible with any scheme of fairness or with any belief in a plan in the universe. We have lost our faith. We were fairly regular temple goers before Charlotte died, but Carson has never set foot in the temple since her death. He says he can't reconcile a loving God with the loss of his young daughter.

I've been back once or twice only when they have a special service that our family always participated in.

Anger

A friend talks:

One of my closest friends just died from AIDS, and I am so angry at the reaction of some members of his family. Near the end Cal had spent all his resources on treatment. He had no insurance, and he was still desperately fighting for his life.

But the attitude of several members of his family was so callous. When Cal asked them to help him financially, they responded by saying, "Are you really sick, or have you just overcharged on your credit cards?" They reminded him of all the times he had gotten into trouble with his money and how they had often helped bail him out. They argued that he wasn't ill. This hurt Cal so much that he severed all relationship with his family. When he finally died, not one member of his family was with him. I am so angry about this that I can't even grieve for Cal. So very, very angry.

The CHOICE for
THE SECOND CRISIS: Stumbling in the Dark

*We can choose to endure
with patience.*

What does it mean to endure with patience? Maya Angelou says in her wonderful poem-book, *Phenomenal Woman*: "All of my work is meant to say, 'You may encounter many defeats but you must not be defeated.' In fact, the encountering may be the very experience which creates the vitality and the power to endure." When we experience a loss, we have definitely had, to use Maya Angelou's words, an *encounter with defeat*, the defeat of our hopes, expectations, dreams, and attempts to make a shape of love and care with our lives.

The choice of this experience of Stumbling in the Dark—to choose to endure with patience—is captured for me in the haunting words of an folk song that was part of my pre-school years spent in the pine woods of South Georgia. I learned this song from Annie, whom I held as my special friend. As Annie helped my mother, who was expecting my little sister Barbara, with the work of the house, Annie sang, her voice low and moaning: "You gotta walk that lonesome road; gotta take that trip through the long, long vale...." Even a four-year-old could hear the accumulated pain, hardship, sadness—and courage—captured in that song. I loved Annie.

It was someone as special as Annie who taught me that I, too, could make the choice to endure with patience, only this time her name was Thornell. The granddaughter of slaves and the mother of a daughter who was a computer specialist and a son who had a Ph.D. degree, Thornell modeled what it meant to choose to endure. I would sit with her for hours, listening to her stories. In those stories I saw my own way forward, even long before I could take the steps. I saw that it is possible to live through terrible times, to refuse to give up, to refuse to become bitter, but, instead, to find the courage to do what you have to do.

Thornell was evidence for me of the truth of the old quotation, "There is a strength of quiet endurance as significant of courage as the most daring feats of prowess." Her ability to endure was a point of light in my dark night. Her actions said to me, "Yes, I have been hit hard. I am hurt. I don't know how everything is going to work out. But I do know this: *I will endure.*"

What helps while I am enduring with patience during THE SECOND CRISIS:

- Journal, paint, garden, build a birdhouse
- Exercise, take nature walks, get a medical checkup
- Pray (If you want to pray but can't, spend time with a person who can)
- Continue to ask others for what you need
- Work with a professional who can be a partner and guide in this dark time
- Talk to a wise person about the "eternal questions" haunting you
- Eat good food
- Slow down
- Spend time with others who express love and concern for you

OBSERVATION:

Linking Past to Present

"I'm going to be in the city to meet with my publisher," I told his secretary on the phone. "I'd like to make an appointment to see Mr. DiMele."

Armand DiMele was the therapist I had visited when I was in New York just a few weeks after Greg's death. After a friend in the city had recommended him to me—"Have you thought about seeing someone who can help you through this?…I know a man who is excellent and who has worked a lot with people who are grieving"—I had gone to see Armand several times during those early critical weeks.

It had been Armand who had told me about the phonograph album that I played night after night when I could not go to sleep. "Jean-Michel Jarre's 'Oxygene,'" he said. "Buy it. Perhaps the sound of that music can give you some sense of life in another dimension."

It was Armand who had given me a special present. The last time I had seen him before returning to Tennessee, he held out a small object. "See, Elizabeth," he said as he showed me the tiny glass figurine, "we have to be whatever we are at any given time in our lives, even when we are wounded. We have to live that moment on the way to other moments." He handed me a beautiful crystal bird. One wing had been broken.

I suppose I expected something similar from Armand when I saw him this time—wisdom offered with gentleness and indirection. But today he did not speak the way he had in the past. His words were sharp and straight.

I began by speaking of my feeling lost and without direction, of loss and tragedy; Armand responded by speaking of the limits of human perception.

"How do you know death is a tragedy?" he asked me. "For people who die, it may not be a tragedy at all. They may be far happier than they were here on earth—who can say? Those of us left here certainly don't know. It may well be," he concluded, "that tragedy is something only the living imagine."

When I spoke of my desperate desire to find something or someone that would make me happy, Armand spoke of the futility of my efforts:

"You will never be so happy again," he warned me. "You will never be so innocent and trusting. You will never know anyone else who will love you the way Greg did. You may," he said, "meet someone to love and be loved by, but you will then be a different person. You will never be able to repeat what you had with Greg. You might as well stop looking. The only place you are going to find happiness is within you."

When I spoke of the impossibility of living without Greg, Armand spoke of actions to be taken:

"Invite a friend to go to dinner tonight. And have this as a rule: Don't mention Greg once during the evening."

I spoke of the emptiness and loneliness of every day, and Armand challenged:

"Well, Elizabeth, what are you going to do about that?"

When I said I wanted my life the way it used to be, he asked:

"Are you going to be like the person I met the other day whose husband has been dead twenty-eight years and she has never taken one item of his clothing from the closet or changed one item in their bedroom? It would be amusing if it weren't so tragic. Because she keeps wondering why she can't get over her sadness. She's such a lonely and unhappy person."

"Oh, I could tell you stories, Elizabeth," Armand went on to say, "of grieving people who attempted to lose themselves in causes—or in excessive care of others. Of those who have retreated to a safe environment and settled for so much less than they had dreamed of for their lives. People who have given up their zest for living and exist in resignation. Many avoid new relationships; if they don't care for anyone, perhaps they will never be hurt again. Some give up all their ideals and beliefs, some withdraw from life, some—"

"But I can't see that I have done any of those things," I said defensively. "What am I hiding behind in order not to have to get on with living?"

"What do you think?" he asked me.

We sat in silence for several seconds. I knew it was time for an honest appraisal.

OBSERVATION: Linking Past to Present

What is normal?
- Reviewing both the positive and negative related to the past
- Sense of gaining some distance
- Dealing with anger, guilt, and blame; forgiving
- Having insights that give meaning to what has been experienced
- Taking stock, especially of reactions and responses to this loss
- Considering priorities
- Coming to rely more on oneself

- Choosing quietness and solitude
- Recognizing truths about your experience of grieving
- Reminiscing, sifting through memories

Responding to loss requires that we review the relationship, mull it over in memories, dreams, fantasies. This review is at the nub of dealing with our loss, for it allows an update of our mental maps of ourselves and our world. This allows us to begin to adjust our mental map to include the reality of the loss. We scan our memory banks to see what is still relevant to our lives and what is not. We find ways to relate to the lost person that allow her or him to continue to be a part of our lives in an appropriate way. We ask, "What do I have to let go of? What can I keep that nurtures me and supports me when I think about the future?"

Listen to these stories:

An Opportunity to Unhook From Anger

A man describes an important realization:

When everything was over and I was living alone, I was so angry. Finally, I realized that the anger was destroying me. So I began a conscious effort; it was not something you do like slice a piece of cake, or at least for me it wasn't. I'd have to repeat: "Don't let that anger ruin your life." I'd say, "Look, anger is anger; it's an emotion, and it's just stored in a closet in your mind; and you let it out, and it does all kinds of cruel and mean things to you."

When worse comes to worst, and I can't get rid of the anger any other way, I go out to the flower beds and start digging up weeds. The ground is really dry, and there are lots of clods. I have this brick wall around my backyard. So, if I'm so angry that I can't talk myself out of it, I pick up those clods and swing them as hard as I can. They just explode when they hit the wall. I confess, sometimes I even get to talking to those weeds and those clods: "Okay, you so and so," I'll say, "you're going next—just hold on, you're going next!" I tell you, I'm killing weeds! I'm breaking clods! And what worked out so well when I threw the clods against the brick wall is that they fell back into the flower beds as soil!

An Acknowledgement of Ambivalent Feelings
A young widow discloses:

I don't know if we would have made it or not. He died in December, and since October we had talked about getting a divorce. I told him I could not stand the way he tried to dominate me. He had to be the macho husband, and he wanted me to be the sweet little wife. I wanted to finish high school, and he didn't want me to. I wanted to have a career; and he said, by damn, he was the breadwinner. We were headed for some change—either through counseling or divorce—and I doubt that it would have been counseling.

So now that he is dead I feel two ways. I'm sad and lonely; I miss him more than I ever thought I would. But sometimes I'm relieved and, I guess you would say, even grateful. In some ways I am lucky that he died because now I am my own person. I can live my life to the fullest. But, you know, even saying that makes me think something bad will happen to me. You're aren't supposed to feel that way about the death of your husband; but it is the way I do feel.

A Recognition of Ways the Lost Person Continues To Be Present
A granddaughter recounts a realization:

The morning after my grandmother died, my husband wrote a little dedication for her and put it by my coffee cup at breakfast. It read: "For Grandmother, I'd wear jogging shorts and a New York Mets cap." I knew why he said this. My grandmother at seventy-nine was active beyond most people's imagination. She had just recently finished painting the outside of her house herself, even managing to fall—with no repercussions—into the kitchen through the back window when the concrete blocks slipped out from under her. She was also an avid Mets fan who would take her portable radio to bed with her when they were playing on the West Coast so she could follow the game, even though it was two o'clock in the morning.

I missed Grandmother after she died; she had been such a spirited presence in our family. Then one day I noticed something: I had started buying stationery and cards that had beautiful flowers on them. ""Ah," I said to myself, "that's Grandmother!" Grandmother always had flowers in her yard, and these flowers were always a topic of conversation when you were with her. I would say that she and flowers were so connected in our family that you couldn't say one without thinking of the other. I had also begun to write to my family, who live in different parts of the country, every week instead of my usual once or twice a month. Grandmother wrote all the children in the family every week, no matter what, and chided the rest of us when we were with her for not "keeping up the family tradition," as she put it. "Family is important," she would say, "You must write to your family."

So without realizing it, I had started doing what Grandmother said—"keeping up the family tradition." This was comforting to me, because I knew this was a way that Grandmother was still present in my life. She will never go away as long as there is flowered stationery and family letters!

The CHOICE for
OBSERVATION: Linking Past to Present

*We can choose to look
honestly.*

This is a choice that requires enormous courage. It requires us to be alone with our thoughts; to focus on our responses rather than on the event of the loss itself; to remember in a balanced way rather than to remember only the good or only the bad; to admit the cost of guilt and anger and be willing to forgive. Anne Morrow Lindberg once said that if suffering made one wise, everyone in the world would be wise. But it takes looking honestly, not just suffering, to make us wise.

The choice to look honestly requires us to call a moratorium on what we may have been doing to "cope" with the loss—things like losing ourselves in our work, involving ourselves excessively in the care of others (usually others we perceive as weaker than we are), running constantly, dwelling obsessively on the past, depending on sleep, drugs, alcohol, television, spending money, or partying to ease our pain. Instead of these, we choose now to grapple with the only questions that can led to wisdom: What meaning does this loss have in my life? How am I choosing to respond to what has happened? How do I intend to act in the future? These are questions of import, questions of power.

This Linking Past to Present is not a time of acceptance. In fact, acceptance is the booby prize in the active grieving process because most people, when asked their definition of *acceptance*, will indicate that the words means something like *resignation*. OBSERVATION, instead, is a time of "living in the question;" of forgiving oneself, others, and life; of noticing how the loss has changed us, altered our environment, scattered our past. It is a period of keeping open the active grieving process in order to have time to think, to experience. It is a time of ambiguity as well as a time of clarity; a time of not knowing and a time of wonderment.

What helps while I am looking honestly during OBSERVATION:

- Spend time alone, reflecting and reminiscing
- Look at photograph albums; relive events of the past
- Work through any debilitating, recurring emotions like guilt, blame, and anger
- Go to places important to you and the lost person
- Think about things you might want to do in the future
- Consider what values, dreams, things that made meaning in the past which you would like to bring forward into the present
- Make scrapbooks
- Write stories about the past that you can share with family and friends
- Recognize the deep value of solitude
- Review the good from the past and the bad
- Sift through memories

THE TURN:

Turning Into the Wind

At Easter I went to Greece. A friend I worked with invited me to go home with her to visit her family.

Chrysoula's parents live on the island of Crete on the outskirts of the town of Kania, where Mr. Bouyotopoulos runs a small wood-working business. The rest of the family—uncles, aunts, cousins, grandfather—live in Vlatos, the ancestral village, high in the mountains at the end of the island. "A very simple life," Chrysoula told me, "raising goats and tending olive trees. Nobody has much, but when I go there I find it hard to leave."

Chrysoula's family spent every Easter with Mr. Bouyotopoulos's father in the ancestral village. Papa Bouyotopoulos, seventy-seven and a widower for many years, prided himself on his self-sufficiency. It was he who always prepared dinner every Easter, a family tradition.

Mr. Bouyotopoulos parked the car in the sandy square of the small village. "Papa lives further up the mountain," Chrysoula told me. "We have to walk from here."

We twisted back and forth on the trail for almost an hour, walking silently, single file. Then, suddenly, the path ended. We were there. In front of us was a small yard surrounded by orange and lemon trees. A kitchen table, set with bowls ready for soup, occupied the center of the open area. "We can never all get into Papa's kitchen,"

Chrysoula said, laughing, "so we always eat out under the trees."

Papa must have heard us coming; for when we stepped into the yard, he was standing at the table breaking eggs. "When you make lamb and rice soup," Mrs. Bouyotopoulos explained, "the egg yolks always have to be whipped at the very last minute."

"Oh, and when you taste it..." Chrysoula added, turning her eyes toward the heavens.

We ate the soup, while the aunts worried about us. Papa was busy removing the young goat from the spit where it had been roasting at the edge of the yard. He brought it to the table and began the carving. When we finished the soup, we ate the succulent meat with its crisp, almost-burnt edges pressed between pieces of thick, coarse bread and washed it down with pungent homemade retsina.

As I sat there—simple, satisfying food in front of me, hospitable, generous people around me—I felt the blackness lifting. I looked across at Papa and his two sisters, each bereft of a partner but clearly relishing being alive. I looked down at the sun-backed earth beneath my feet and then up toward the blue patches of sky that were showing through the orange and lemon trees. Suddenly I felt a shift occur in my body; there was an actual physical alteration. Something released inside me. This shift was immediately followed by an inexplicable sense of well-being, of calmness and serenity. The vague foreboding—the sense that "something is not right; something bad is about to happen," which had been a constant presence in my life since Greg's death—had left me. Instead, sitting there as if in a round of sky and trees and light and earth, I felt in touch with something elemental, strong, ineffable. In touch with what seemed at that moment all one would ever need to know, with something deeply healing.

After dinner, it became clear that Papa had plans. "He wants us to go with him up the mountain; he has something he wants to show us," Chrysoula told me. We followed the spry old man, who was carrying two wooden buckets filled with water, as he led us to a path that seemed to go straight up the mountain. We climbed for many minutes.

Then we turned a final curve in the path. Ahead was what Papa had brought us to see. Planted in the large clearing were hundreds of tiny oak seedlings. Row after row of little trees lined the steep hillside, narrow furrows plowed between them. It was Papa's forest. He proceeded carefully to water every tiny tree.

I stood there in amazement, looking first at Papa and then at the hillside of seedlings. I could imagine the amount of work this project required: how the old man's back must hurt from all the bending and how his arms must ache from hauling water up the mountain.

"Why would he do this?" I asked myself. "This is a man seventy-seven years old. He cannot possibly live long enough to see these seedlings become a forest." Chrysoula's mother seemed to read my mind, for she turned and said, "Papa has planted these trees as part of a reclamation program sponsored by an environmentalist organization active here on the island. 'For the land,' he says. 'So the family will always have trees on the land.'"

I thought about this all the way down the path as we walked back to our car at the end of the visit. Seeing Papa Bouyotopoulos's forest had deeply stirred me. I didn't quite know what it was that had touched me so, but it had something to do with making a contribution that will live on after you, something about looking out at life instead of always obsessively staring inward. I knew the experience had made an opening in my thinking. Because for the first time since Greg's death, I found myself considering the idea that there might be projects worth doing in life, some commitments worth making.

THE TURN: Turning Into the Wind

What is normal?

- Gaining an awareness that our responses to the loss, if not changed, will hold us back from enjoying life
- Recognizing that only we can begin the longer-term adjustive tasks that must be engaged in if we are to make a new life for ourselves
- Becoming willing to stop focusing on the past
- Becoming willing to take responsibility for our own happiness and well being
- Starting to reconstitute our current belief system and explore our deep values
- Finding ways to express our feelings for the lost person that are appropriate now
- Assessing our critical role in what kind of life we will have in the future

When I asked people dealing with loss to describe the insights and actions that characterize THE TURN for them, they reported:

Making a Decision to Turn from Loss to Living

A senior citizen whose sister had died asserts:

It has taken me a while, but I've decided life is worth doing anyway. Because you have to live until you die, so you might as well perk up. Attitude is everything. The hardest thing to do after a loss is to know when to say, "I've grieved enough." It's hard to time. But you do get to the place where you know you have a choice. I mean, if you're a living, breathing, semiconscious person, you realize finally that you have to make the choice to have enough nerve to do something.

Recognizing Continuity

A widow recalls:

We took Akio's ashes back to Japan the year after he died. That was when I got a sense that life itself has continuity—in spite of the death of individuals. We went to central Japan to the place where Akio's parents are buried. Actually, it's the family graveyard, and there's a temple that has been the family temple for centuries.

We had a burial service at this family temple, and then we walked to the graveyard and the Buddhist priest put the ashes in the stone.

I felt a deep calm after the ceremony. For me, Akio was now part of that temple that had been there for centuries and, as far as I know, will be there for centuries long after I am gone. I got a real sense that life started before we were born and will go on afterward. For me, this was very peaceful.

When I got home, I found myself building on that sense of continuity. I became very clear that I wanted to keep up the Japanese side of my life. I am an America, but Akio and I were married for over twenty-five years and I have been greatly enriched by the Japanese people and culture.

So I said to myself when I got back from Japan. "I'm not going to lose all that." So I read about Japanese things. I keep myself abreast of the culture. This is providing me continuity.

Deciding Not to Be a Victim

A woman told this story:

One day I said to myself, "Sally, you've pined long enough. Get up from this couch and make yourself some clothes. You've got to go out and get a job." So I began to sew. As soon as I had a couple of outfits made, I decided it was time to start looking for work. I had contacted my friends and said, "If you hear of anything, let me know." So now it was "Sally, get ready. It's time to take yourself out into the world because no one else is going to do it for you."

The CHOICE For
THE TURN: Turning Into the Wind

We can choose to replan and change our life to include but not be dominated by the loss.

This choice to replan our lives to include the loss we have had is an assertion, a declaration, something we just affirm without knowing what the exact outcome is going to be. We are now "stating or putting forward an assertion positively, even if in the face of difficulties." We are proclaiming that we will go forward; we will incorporate this loss into our lives in a way that does not keep us stuck in the past but provides us a way forward into the future.

John Bowlby warns us: If we choose not to begin to "replan our lives the representational models we have of ourselves and of the world about us remain unchanged: and we subsequently find that "our life is either planned on a false basis or else falls into unplanned disarray."

The choice to replan our lives is first and foremost an internal commitment, a private decision: *I will contribute to my own rehabilitation. I will make necessary changes. I will build something new for the future.* The internal commitment comes first; then some kind of external action will naturally and appropriately follow.

I don't think it is too dramatic to say that this choice is a life-or-death issue. We will either make an assertion that we are committed to shaping a new life that includes the past but is also expanding, shaping a new life that is appropriate for who we are now and our current circumstances— or we will live, in the words of that old French saying, as a person whose clock has stopped. (The Institute of Medicine says it this way: "Not only is there no movement, but there also is a sense that the person will not permit any movement.")

People who don't make the choice to replan their lives at the appropriate time after a loss have sad fates: some become chronic mourners; some continue destructive behavior; some lose themselves in work and frantic activity; some continue delinquent behavior; some continue to be ill; some sink into chronic depression; and some die. There are also the "hidden" aftermath of not making the choice to replan and change one's life to include but not be identified by the change, outcomes that probably do relate to grieving not being complete but which may not be seen as being directly connected. Some people who choose not to commit to the longer-term changes may "feel deeply dissatisfied with their lives; may become super self-sufficient; many feel depersonalized with a sense of unreality." They exist as what Donald Winnicott calls a "false self." Many are angry and bitter. They become brittle and hard, having "little understanding either of others or of themselves, difficult to live and work with."

What helps while I am replanning my life during THE TURN:

- Take proactive steps to show a commitment to making a new shape for your life
- Make positive and appropriate changes in your environment
- Make collages that show how you would like your life to be in the future
- Write to explore new possibilities for your life
- Organize your affairs
- Assert to yourself and to others that you are responsible for creating a life appropriate to the person you are now and the situation in which you find yourself now

RECONSTRUCTION:

Picking Up the Pieces

The surf was so strong that I had to turn up the volume on the cassette player under my lounge chair. Taking advantage of the lull between the summer and fall semesters at the university, I had invited my parents to join me at this isolated spot on the coast of North Carolina.

The first task of the morning was to set up my "work area"—make sure the rickety side table was close enough to the lounge chair so I could reach my coffee, stack up the cassette boxes on the sand in a certain order, put out my books, pen, and writing tablet.

Haydn's 100th Symphony was playing, and I was reading Anne Morrow Lindbergh's *Gift From The Sea*. This was not a book I had brought with me but one I had found in the bookcase of the cottage. Greg had been reading *Gift From The Sea* on the afternoon he died; the book was lying on his work table, one passage marked to include in the manuscript on which he was working. It had made me happy to find the book here at the beach because Greg, never far from my thoughts in the entire fifteen months since his death, had been on my mind a lot since we had arrived here.

I recognized the passage he had planned to use when I came to it. "But I want first of all...to be at peace with myself...an inner harmony, essentially spiritual, which can be translated into outer harmony." This passage struck me again, as it had when I first read it, as the perfect epitaph. If Greg had known he was going to die, I thought to myself, he couldn't have picked a more appropriate final testimony.

But today there was something else about these words…I couldn't put my finger on why, but reading the paragraph today bothered—even provoked—me.

I put the book down in my lap and looked out at the ocean. A fleet of shrimp boats was passing in the far distance. The scene was mesmerizing: the flat plane of the ocean, the center poles of the boats rising against the horizon, the high booms turning first left and then right as the nets were moved into the water. As I watched, I realized…what was it? Ah, the clue was in the geometry. In looking at these lines and angles, I was seeing not only ocean and boats, booms and center poles; I was seeing *harmony.*

Harmony that in my own life was not present.

I looked back at the paragraph. *I want a central core to my life…purity of intention…singleness of eye…I want to be at peace with myself…inner…outer harmony…at one.* Those words stung me. I realized that even though I had turned toward the future, even though I had found a new job that brought me into contact with different people and gave me some diversion, those things were not the same as the "purity of intention" that Anne Morrow Lindbergh was writing about. In spite of these changes, my daily life still had no central core, no true purpose. Where everything meaningful had been when Greg was alive was still only a vacuum.

"Great," I said, slapping the book down on the table. "I'll put it in my schedule: Get meaning in daily life at ten o'clock next Thursday." I was sick and tired of always having to work on something related to Greg's death. When would life feel just like normal living? When would I be through with all this adjusting? I reached down to change the music, putting the Bob Seger tape into the Sony. As I began to gather up my things to go inside, "Against the Wind" was the song that was playing.

The sun was just starting to go down as I headed out to the beach for my daily run. Off and on all day, thoughts about the passage in *Gift From The Sea* had aggravated me; but as I jogged along, seeing the reflection of the strong afternoon light on the wet sand, I began to feel less irritable. A line from Proust came to mind—"If I were dying," he had said, "and the sun made a patch of light on the floor, my spirit would rise in happiness." It made me happy to remember that quotation.

It was then that the idea occurred to me. One way I could start building harmony in my daily life would be to change my home environment. I could move furniture, paint the walls another color...why, I could even put in a skylight! The thought made me feel almost giddy. Even as I jogged, I could see the light streaming into my den, making moving patterns on the ceramic tile floor. By the time I got back to the beach cottage, the skylight was already installed and I was sitting under it.

RECONSTRUCTION: Picking Up the Pieces

What is normal?
- Beginning to make changes that are hard but beneficial
- Working to establish a new identity
- Recognizing other issues not directly related to our loss must now be dealt with
- Making commitments to new projects

- Distinguishing between the loneliness we can do something about—loneliness of social isolation—and the loneliness that can be assuaged only by some "reaffiliation" that brings deep emotional connection
- Developing new skills
- Setting new priorities
- Acknowledging that in our grieving we are now engaging in long-term tasks of adjustment and change which are difficult and take time

This is a time of paradox. On the one hand, we begin to feel alive again, to feel enthusiastic. We no longer live every moment of the day in the slough of despondency. At the same time, we are confronted by the blank canvas of our future. We do not know what to recommit to. We do not know how we are going to reestablish our life purpose. We are unclear about our direction.

Individuals report RECONSTRUCTION: Picking Up the Pieces experiences like these:

Looking At The Future

A widower says:

I work as a historian at a research center where we write many grant proposals. When one proposal isn't funded, we sit down and write another one. I've started thinking about my life as a widower as something I have to write a new proposal for. But, in a case like this, I don't know yet what kind of proposal to write. I have to do a lot of searching, and I've begun to do some of that. I wish I knew. It's a most uncomfortable place to be in, not to know what direction your life is going to go in. But from all I can see, being uncomfortable while you think about the future just comes with the territory.

Experiencing Confusion

Listen to this story:

It's a shame to have to say at age thirty-three, "What am I going to be when I grow up?" but the truth is I don't know what to do with the rest of my life. I've sold the business that Jack had. It wasn't something I wanted to run. But I do want to do something. I majored in Russian in college, so maybe I'll go back to graduate school. But I've got to think of the three girls I have to raise. Can you imagine a few years from now having three girls in college at one time. So financial study would also be valuable. How do I choose? What if I make a mistake? You can't make many mistakes at my age and in my circumstances and have it not seriously affect your future and the futures of lots of other people. It just seems too important to make the right decision, but what is that right thing to do? At least I'm thinking about this, but there is still a lot of confusion.

Making Changes

A widow says:

I've made a list of all the things I've been doing out of habit but that I really don't like to do. I've been in a study group for over five years, and it dawned on me the other day that I don't enjoy being there. I've also been in a tennis league for a long time. I realized lately that I was in that activity because some of my friends were participating but that I didn't enjoy tennis. So I've canceled both of those activities and signed up to take a genealogy class at the community college. That's something I've been wanting to do for a long time. I think I've hesitated to make changes like this, thinking that a widow needs to keep doing things with her friends as much as possible. But I realized the other day that a widow can also decide what she likes to do on her own account and do that. I've felt better ever since.

The CHOICE for
RECONSTRUCTION: Picking Up the Pieces

*We can choose to take
specific actions.*

John Bowlby says it this way: we now have a choice to begin "active interchange between ourselves and our external world." When we are involved in this active interchange, he reminds us, we are in the process of organizing our lives toward some new goal or object. This activity will likely result, as the stories in this chapter have shown us, in a mix of subjective experience—"hope, fear, anger, satisfaction, frustration, or any combination of these...." But no matter how much we go back and forth, up and down, during this interim, we are still moving forward. By taking action—which inevitably involves risking changes, some which work out and some of which don't—we are finding out what it will take for our lives to be satisfying. We are "trying out" alternatives to see what will be the appropriate shape for our new future.

The choice to take specific actions will result in "contradictory drives toward maturity and regression." This is unavoidable, because we are in a new situation. "All the usual responses are completely out of tune and inadequate to meet it." Therefore, our behavior "becomes unpredictable." As Lily Pincus says pointedly, "It is not just losing a state in which one had found one's balance, but rather as if one has lost one's balanced self. In attempting to regain it, one may try out some new ways of coping, giving up certain wishes, defining a new task."

This is what happens during RECONSTRUCTION. We begin the work to make the replanning of our lives not just an idea but a reality. We begin the work necessary to design and create a new shape for our lives. To gain a new balanced self, we "try out" new ways of living. We initiate an "active interchange" with the external world.

What helps while I am taking new actions during RECONSTRUCTION

- Take specific steps to learn new skills that you recognize you now need
- Work with a career counselor, a life coach, or a group of individuals who are committed to making life-enhancing changes
- Stop doing things that only remind you of the past
- Make new friends
- Talk to someone about any emotional pain, sadness, fear, and sense of helplessness that might recur as you begin to construct a new future

WORKING THROUGH:

Finding Solid Ground

It was past midnight when I arrived in San Francisco. I was very tired when I finally reached the hotel and planned to fall into bed immediately. These plans changed, however, when I walked into my room. For the first thing I saw, lying on the desk, was the new textbook Greg and I had been writing when he died.

I leafed through the book. It was so exciting to see what had once been scribbled on yellow legal paper now appearing as printed words on the page. I felt like a kid at Christmas. The fatigue had all left me.

Then a piece of folded paper fell out of the book. "Call me no matter what time you get in," the note read. "All I can say is, 'I'm sorry.'" It was signed by my editor.

"Have you seen the book?" was Robert's first question.

"Yes," I answered. "I love it. It's so beautiful."

There was a long pause. "Well, have you noticed the second color?…."

"The second color?" I echoed. "No, I didn't pay any attention to the second color. Is something wrong with it?" I was turning as fast as I could to find a page with a second color.

"Yes, something is wrong," Robert answered. "The second color isn't the warm brown we specced. It's purple!"

Now I saw. All the headings in the book, all the explanations under the drawings, everywhere color had been used for emphasis…all of these were *bright* purple.

"Well," I said quickly, trying to toss the mistake off lightly. "I bet English teachers will love purple for a change. The color will get the book a lot of attention."

There was a long pause, and then Robert said. "Elizabeth, this is really serious. Our marketing department spent several thousand dollars doing research to determine the best second color for this book…you know that many of the ideas in the book are innovative, so it was critical that the design and color be traditional. This bright purple trivializes the book, makes it look trendy. We'll never be able to sell it in the conservative English market."

I did see the gravity of the situation. And I was getting angry. "Well, what happened?" I asked, realizing that my voice was several decibels louder. "How, after all that research and planning, did we end up with a book with purple as the second color?"

"It was a clerical error," Robert answered. "Someone confused two orders as the book was going to press."

I just stood there, holding the phone for a few seconds, trying to think of something to say. But there was nothing. Robert's voice was low as he closed the conversation. "I really am sorry, Elizabeth," he said. "Everyone in the company is sick about the mistake. But the book is dead. All we can do now is try to cut our losses." I knew what that meant. No special sales thrust. No special advertising. Everybody trying to forget the book instead of trying to sell it.

I cried for hours. I had never felt so defeated. But at some point, something snapped in me. "I will not have it be this way," I said defiantly. "I will not have it. Too much work and effort have gone into this project for such a miserable ending."

Ten o'clock found me on Union Square waiting for the doors to be unlocked at I. Magnin's. I headed straight for the men's department. "I want to buy some purple shirts," I said to the salesman. "Solid purple."

If he had said there were no men's shirts in solid purple, I was already prepared with an alternate plan. But plan B turned out not be necessary, for the gentleman said, "Let's go over to the sportswear department. Pierre Cardin has designed some solid-colored shirts this year in bright colors, and one of them is purple."

It was probably the most purple shirt I will ever see. I could not imagine anyone in normal circumstances buying it. "It's a little bright," the salesman said tentatively, "but it's the only thing we have in purple."

"I'll take two," I said without hesitating, "one large and one medium. I'd like them gift-wrapped," I added.

Everyone was at the booth when I walked into the exhibit area. The national sales manager was there, as well as my editor. "I have something for you," I said, handing each of them a box containing the shirt.

"Do you want us to open these now?" the men all asked me. They seemed a little pleased but mostly awkward.

"Yes," I responded. "Now is the time to open them."

It was one of those situations where the gift is so bad that it's wonderful. These were not men who wore loud purple shirts. These were men who wore wing-tipped shoes and conservative button-down collars. That, of course, made these shirts all the more ridiculous.

At first the men did not know how to react. Were they supposed to like these? Were they supposed to show their appreciation? But then, first one and then the next began to laugh. Soon all of us standing around this serious college textbook publisher's booth were laughing. Bending-over-double laughing. Holding-the-shirts-up-in-front-of-themselves laughing.

Suddenly the color purple had lost its heaviness, its significance. One could even imagine, standing there, that these men might be able to sell a new college textbook to a conservative market, even if it did have a second color that was purple.

The next few days proved that supposition to be accurate. The reps had good reports; professors liked the books; many said they would be ordering. I knew that by the time the news of this success at the national convention reached the entire sales force, the book would stand a good chance of being heavily promoted. Naturally, this made me happy. But I was also mentally and physically exhausted. I had no idea that a person had to work this hard to create a new shape for living.

WORKING THROUGH: Finding Solid Ground

What is normal?
- Experiencing new problems related to changes we are making
- Practicing new roles
- Dealing with breakdowns and finding creative solutions
- Risking
- Determining how to respond to disappointments and adversity resulting from new activities and new commitments
- Continuing to develop a new identity consistent with who we are now and what our life circumstances are now
- Re-examining assumptions
- Realizing the need for self-management
- Reconstituting and reaffirming values and beliefs

People have described this cluster of experiences of working through in these stories:

Reactivation of Fears

A young mother relates this story:

Only someone who has ever had a firstborn die a crib death can know what it takes to decide to have another baby. Right before Kimberly was born, I dreamed again and again about Tommy's death. That made me afraid something was wrong with the baby I was carrying. We didn't even talk about the possibility of crib death, just whether or not she would have all her fingers and toes—would she have anything wrong with her.

Even though it's highly unlikely that a second baby in a family will die of crib death, we still keep Kimberly hooked up to a monitor. The fear is residue left over from Tommy's death, I know. One day when Kimberly was about three months old, the monitor's beeper went off. It's customary for babies to breathe irregularly at times; and if the monitor beeps, you're supposed to stand there and count to ten to see if the baby corrects herself, which is what is normal. My first thought, of course, was that she was dead; and it was the hardest thing in the world to stand there and count to ten to see if she started breathing again. I knew I had to, though; I had to face that fear. In just a few seconds everything was back to normal. That experience has given me the courage to take her off the monitor more often.

Bringing Meaning From The Past
Into A New Form In The Present

A widow told this story:

Family was always so important to my husband and me. His four brothers and their wives would come to see us, all at the same time, and we would have such a good time together.

I enjoyed cooking for them—"the old-fashioned way," they called it. I enjoyed every minute—making biscuits for every meal, bowls of cream gravy, fried pork chops.

After my husband died, we didn't have family events like that anymore. We were all still close, but we just didn't visit the way we did before. I really missed that experience of "family." Then I discovered one day that writing about the past put me back in touch with all those good feelings. I wrote a little vignette about my childhood—about the day my papa's drugstore burned down—and although it was simple and might not be to others great writing, I really enjoyed it. So I began putting together a collection of stories from the past, which I gave to all the family one Christmas.

The funny thing was that to write those stories I ended up visiting every one of the four brothers to get facts and details. It was a new way to enjoy family.

Dealing With Surprises

A widow talks:

It took me about three years—I remained a part of a grief support group in my parish this entire time—to move far enough in my grieving process to decide it was time to sell the family home. My husband and I had lived in the same house for over fifty years. All of our eight children were born and grew up when we were living there. So it wasn't easy to part with the house and a lot of the furnishings.

But I loved the condo I bought. It was light and airy, with an atrium tall enough for me to grow trees! Now it was time for the first Thanksgiving since I had moved into my new place. All the children and all the grandchildren were coming for dinner as they did every year.

I bought the turkey and the ham and planned the dishes: baked squash casserole, sweet potatoes with marshmallows broiled on top, stuffing (both with and without oysters—to

44

please everybody). The day before Thanksgiving when I started preparing the food was the first time I realized that in this new condo I did not have two ovens. I had always had two ovens; it had been a necessity to have two ovens with our large family. Now I had only one oven—a small one at that— and there was no way I could prepare all this food and have it ready on time with only one oven.

This situation caught me completely off guard. I began to castigate myself for making the move. I felt I had made the biggest mistake in the world. I was distraught.

Then I thought, "I love this place. Surely there is some way I can solve the problem." I called the condo manager and asked if the club house kitchen were available. "On Wednesday before Thanksgiving? You bet. It's completely open." So my dilemma was solved. I made up all the food and then sent family members down the street to the club house when it was time for baking what I couldn't fit into my own oven. We still laugh about that. It's a whole new set of memories.

The CHOICE for
WORKING THROUGH: Finding Solid Ground

*We can choose to engage
in the conflicts.*

Conflict, we are told, "is a very powerful organizing principle of behavior, simplifying and clarifying immediate purposes." As we weigh pros and cons, look for solutions, grapple with issues, we are, in effect, determining our values, setting our priorities, deciding on what is and is not acceptable to us. We are drawing the contours of our future.

Choosing to engage in the conflicts of this phase of active grieving makes our internal grief more manageable. By engaging with the difficulties and problems that have resulted from the loss and from our commitment to reconstruct our lives after that loss, we have an arena where, by trial and error, we can work through our grieving.

What helps while I am engaging with the conflicts during WORKING THROUGH:

- Seek out people who are proficient at what needs to be learned
- Focus on solving problems rather than being upset that the problems are there
- Distinguish problems related to the loss from those that are just part of living
- Replenish yourself—sitting still, taking walks, writing poems, looking at art you love, listening to music, cooking new recipes, gardening, fishing, getting massages
- Be patient

INTEGRATION:

Daylight

As the months passed, I felt more and more centered in my work: I felt that by focusing on writing books I had reconnected with what gave me meaning and purpose.

But I couldn't feel that way about other areas, particularly about my personal life. What I had shared with Greg had been like a destination, the place I had dreamed about all my life, the place I most wanted to get to. So what was there to reconnect with there? Nothing. So even when my work was going well, I still had to fight off depressing feelings of "What's the use?" Everything was still so empty; I was so lonely. What was I to do with the memories of a man I loved who no longer existed in human form?

Then came the dream and the student's letter.

The dream was simple. There was a large green plant that had been thrown aside on the lawn. But when I picked the plant up I made a wonderful discovery. The plant had roots! I knew in the dream that the plant could be repotted and would stay alive. The discovery in the dream made me deliriously happy.

A few days later I received a letter from one of Greg's former graduate students with whom I had not had contact since shortly after Greg died. Chuck wrote:

Greg was the first person close to me who ever died. He was my mentor, the teacher I wanted to be. And he just passed right out of

47

my life. He went out so quickly, so irretrievable, so irrevocably. I couldn't go to the funeral, so I didn't get a chance to say good-bye. I did say good-bye one night out in the backyard of my house, but things still always seemed unfinished.

But something happened recently that allowed me to see the place Greg has and will always have in my life. It happened as I was completing a writing seminar prior to taking my doctoral orals.

Then the student told the story. Dr. Graves, the professor in the writing seminar, had instructed the graduate students: "Read Scott Momaday's tribute to his grandmother—'Now that I can have her only in memory, I see my grand-mother....standing at the wood stove on a winter morning and turning meat in a great iron skillet; sitting at the south window, bent over her beadwork....' Then write a model of Momaday's paragraph, using someone as the subject whom you can have now only in memory."

The student told me he had chosen Greg, and that this was what he had written:

Now that I can only have Greg in memory, I recall the sense of continuity that was shattered when he fell off a road in East Tennessee and out of all our lives forever. I think of Greg and I see Kris Kristofferson, grizzled beard, deep voice, sparkling, deep-set eyes. He was my teacher, my colleague, my friend, who showed me how to step across a boundary and leave all the tangled messes behind. It was the crossing that mattered.

Once we were going into a Japanese restaurant. You had to cross a little bridge to get to it. Greg was bothered by something that had happened at the university. I didn't know what it was, but something had disturbed him. As we started to go into the restaurant, Greg said, "When I go across this bridge, I'm leaving the problem here and I'm going over there. It's not going to be with me anymore, and we're going to go ahead and have our time together."

We did have a wonderful time, and it was one of my greatest lessons in life, watching Greg do that. What he taught me was to let go of things and move on. I think that's why I had such a hard time letting go of him—because he taught me how to let go and I couldn't imagine letting go of that. Continuity. The smooth movement from here to there, from then to now, and on into tomorrow without getting caught in any one place too long. That's what he taught me, and it's always with me.

The student ended his letter: *I'm convinced the reason we are here is to remember, if we understand memory to be that uniquely human ability to create from the past a sense of meaning in the present and a trembling anticipation of possibility in the future.*

When I finished Chuck's letter, I knew I had gained wisdom: a person who is gone can live on in memory as an *active* agent in one's life, not just as someone you love and miss, not just as a nostalgic sadness. Greg had been remembered by his student; and that remembering had altered the quality of the student's life in the present and informed his life for the future:...*if we understand memory to be that uniquely human ability to create from the past a sense of meaning in the present and a trembling anticipation of possibility in the future.*

That, I realized, was how a person we love and have lost can remain in our lives forever, in a way that is neither morbid nor regressive. And in a way that honors the lost person at the same time that it makes room for others. *We make meaning* of the memories. From the memories we extract values, ideals, insight, pleasures, awareness.

This, then, was how Greg would fit into my life. I knew, for instance, that I would always care for my family in a different way because Greg had enabled me to see them in a new light. I would always feel more connected to the out-of-doors because with him I had learned new ways to see the woods, the mountains, the sea. I would always be more awake to the sensuous pleasures of life—colors, smells, sounds, tastes—because I had been able to experience it with him. And I would always know what love was because he had loved me. I would always enjoy the opera and ballet, which I first discovered with him. I would always read books about the Lewis and Clark expedition because I had followed the trail with him one summer and caught a glimpse of how that trek symbolizes a journey that is possible for all of us. I would always like red geraniums by the front door and eggs scrambled with brie. I would always want to drive a clean car, and I would always ask if the saltwater taffy had been made on the premises.

I also realized how much I had changed internally. Some entries in my commonplace book clearly marked my commitment to the inner life:

Margareit Yourcenar quoting the philosopher Saint-Martin, who had said about his friends:

They are the beings through whom God loved me.

This seemed to me, as I looked back at my active grieving process, a worthy purpose for a person to now have for her life: to be someone through whom God loved others.

I saw a Howard Thurman quote I had taped next to the words of Yourcenar:

Each of us, in our own way, finds the stairs leading to the Holy Place. We gather in our hands the fragments of our lives, searching eagerly for some creative synthesis, some wholeness, some all-encompassing unity capable of stilling the tempests within us and quieting all the inner turbulence of our fears. We seek to walk in our own path which opens up before us, made clear by the light of [the Divine] Spirit and the radiance which it casts all around us... The assumption is that the individual is ever in immediate candidacy to get an "assist" from God—that she is not alone in her quest. Through prayer, meditation and singleness of mind, the individual's life may be invaded by strength, insight, and courage sufficient for her needs. Thus she need not seek refuge in excuses but can live her life with ever-increasing vigor and experience...an ever-deepening sense of fulfillment.

I knew immediately the reason for this entry in my commonplace book: the quiet time and prayer that I had begun in OBSERVATION had become by now the very context of my life. I knew that the possibility and the promise of a well-tended and honored inner life that focused on partnership with the Holy Other would always now be my first commitment. I continued, as Howard Thurman said, to receive that "assist" from God; I was blessed by being "invaded by strength, insight and courage sufficient" for my needs.

INTEGRATION: Daylight

What is normal?
- Feeling released
- Being able to identify in our lives many of Dr. Frank Kohut's Victorious Outcomes:
  - An enlarged capacity for empathy
  - The ability to think beyond the bounds of the individual
  - A recognition that there has been an increase in one's wisdom
  - A new outlook on life
  - Ability to pay attention to what really matters
  - A kind of "quiet pride" in knowing that human existence is finite
  - Heightened capacity for humor
  - Increased ability to hold life's ups and downs in perspective
- Being able to identify in our lives many of Dr. George Pollock's Creative Outcomes:
  - The ability to feel joy, satisfaction, and a sense of accomplishment

- A return to a steady state of balance
- The experience of an increased capacity to appreciate people and things
- A realization that we are more tolerant and wise
- A desire to express ourselves creatively
- The ability to invest in new relationships
- The experience of a sense of play and freedom
- A deepening of our faith
- Having a clearer sense of what we believe in and what truths we choose to live by
- Looking up and being able to see a horizon

We do not experience these creative outcomes because we have been able to recreate how things were before the loss. What we experience now, because the active grieving process is an adaptive-transformational process, is a "new creation." A new creation that derives "its energy and perhaps inspiration and direction from the past," to be sure, but is nevertheless a "successor" creation, not a replacement. We have been changed by the active grieving process; and, as a result, we have changed things around us.

The women and men with whom I have talked speak of the release and new life that come during the experiences of INTEGRATION: Daylight.

Gaining Perspective

A man says:

You've got to be able to see that this is some sort of learning process and that you don't always know everything that is happening. It's like the old Chinese story of the farmer whose champion stallion ran away and all the neighbors gathered to say, "That's bad." And the old farmer said, "Maybe." The next day the stallion came back with a whole herd of wild horses, and the neighbors all said, "That's good," and the farmer said, "Maybe." Then the farmer's son broke his leg trying to tame one of the wild horses and the neighbors said, "That's bad," and the old farmer said, "Maybe." Right after the son broke his leg, the army came through and drafted all the young men and took them off to war, but they left the farmer's son because his leg was broken. All the neighbors said, "That's good," to which the old farmer only said, "Maybe." And, of course, the story never ends.

That illustrates to me that whatever is happening now, you don't really know what is going on. And I've seen during these years of grief work that this is true. It's a real irony, isn't it, that I would have ended up coming out of this thing an optimist!

Seeing the Glass as Half-Full

A mother says:

I noticed people thought that since I had lost a young child who suffered seven years before she died that I would be very heavy and significant about life. But, the truth is, through the pain I learned that you can be miserable anywhere you want to be and you can be happy anywhere you want to be. It's what you make of yourself.

Once when I lived in Okinawa, it wasn't the best living conditions, and there were wives there who were just miserable. They sat around all day being miserable. Well, hell, anybody can be miserable. It doesn't take much of a person to be sad and miserable. It takes a heck of a person to make the best out of what's the worst. When you go to the commissary and you want butter and they say, "Well, there's no butter; there's not going to be any butter for two weeks." What do you do? You ask, "Well, do you have any whipping cream?" "Yes, we've got whipping cream." So you buy whipping cream and make butter out of whipping dream. Add a little salt and a little yellow food coloring, and you got butter. That's how you should take life. That's what life is. Whipping cream. I learned this by grieving.

Enjoying Being Outrageous

A widow tells this story:

I find that since I've lived through a traumatic experience of loss I prefer lively people. People who are doing things. It's as if surviving and returning to life brings with it a new kind of lightness and freedom. In fact, I don't mind if people are outrageous. I now enjoy being outrageous myself at times. I like people who are willing to take a risk, and being outrageous is taking a risk, isn't it?

About three years after Tom died, I was in England. The fad in London that summer was spraying your hair all kinds of fanciful colors—green, pink, blue, purple. You could wash the paint out; so if you didn't like blue hair, the next day you could try purple or yellow or green.

Well, that fall I had a huge class—225 students in biochemistry—and one day before I went to class I sprayed my hair electric blue with some of that hair paint I had bought in England. I just went into the room—me, this sixty-year-old scientist—and started my lecture. In a few minutes this serious kid sitting in the front row raised his hand and said, "Dr. Williams, why is your hair blue?" I looked him right in the eye and said, "Because I just felt like being outrageous." He continued to look puzzled all during class, but I went right on with my lecture. On the teaching evaluations at the end of the term, several students commented: "That blue hair was marvelous!" Now, can I prove that my ability to have fun like that and my having experienced Tom's death are related? I can't, of course, but I *know* there is a connection.

The CHOICE for INTEGRATION: Daylight

We can choose to continue to make and remake choices.

I think it was Madame de Stael, the eighteenth-century French novelist, who said, "The human mind always make progress, but it is a progress of spirals." This is the way of life, too. And the way of loss. The loss we have just actively grieved represents just one of the innumerable losses we will need to grieve for during our lifetime. In fact, at times, in order to move through the grieving process, we have had to create other losses. When we make changes in order to start to create a new identity, for instance, we often have to leave behind certain activities, habitual ways, even people; and each of these losses starts a mini-process of grieving inside our larger ongoing process. Spirals within spirals.

New losses, too, often reactive earlier losses. Lily Pincus says, "The loss...of an important person strikes at the deepest roots of human existence, recalls the experience of previous attachments and losses, and reactivates the pain of earlier bereavements, physical as well as psychological in nature." Therefore, we have to be willing to continue to make and remake choices that will allow us to experience the *transformational-mourning-liberation process* for all of our resurrected and our future losses.

Recognizing that life does present us with both a repetition and a succession of losses is part of the wisdom we gain as a result of engaging in the full grieving process. We also have a larger context for holding our losses that, while giving them their due, makes them only part of the whole mosaic of our lives, not the total picture.

To be willing to continue to make and remake choices allows us to participate, as Ernest Becker speaks of it, in the "mysterious way in which life is given to us in evolution on this planet…. Who know," he says, "what form the forward momentum of life will take in the time ahead or what use it will make of our anguished searching. The most that any one of us can seem to do is to fashion something—an object or ourselves—and drop it into the confusion, make an offering of it, so to speak, to the life force." We can commit to doing good. We can ask for divine help to be a person through whom God loves those around us. We can contribute to others what we have learned from our grieving. This is reason enough to commit to doing the work that is necessary to move through our losses.

What to do after reaching INTEGRATION: Daylight

- Acknowledge and celebrate the hard work you have accomplished
- Share your wisdom with others
- Honor your sense of humor
- Keep exploring; be adventuresome
- Stay in touch with what gives your life meaning
- Keep some time for stillness and quiet
- Remind yourself, when you face another loss, of what you have learned

EPILOGUE

When I was mourning, William Stafford sent me a poem
he had written called "Rescue," which goes like this:

A fire was burning. In another room
someone was talking. Sunlight slanted
across the foot of my bed, and a glass of water
gleamed where it waited on a chair near my hand.
I was alive and the pain in my head
was gone. Carefully I tried thinking of those I had known.
I let them walk
and then run, and then open their mouths the way
it used to cause the throbbing. It didn't hurt
anymore. Clearer and clearer I stared
far into the glass. I was cured.

From now on in my life there would be a place
like a scene in a paperweight. One figure in the storm
would be reaching out with my hand for those
who had died. It would always be still in that scene,
no matter what happened. I could come back to it,
carefully, any time, to be saved, and go on.

It seems so long ago now, that July afternoon when, driv-
ing along the road to find my husband, I instead found myself
a widow. And today I think I can say that I understand the
poem that Bill sent me.

For there is something redemptive—*"come back to it, care-*
fully, any time, to be saved, and go on"—about the mourning

57

process, something that resides in the power and opportunity we have to make choices. These choices, of course, allow us to make for ourselves a new life in the external. For instance, I now no longer teach school but, instead, write books, consult, speak, and lead retreats. Several years after becoming a widow, I married a wonderful man, Jerele Neeld, with whom I deeply enjoy the adventure of living.

But the real impact, I think, of the choices we make when we are grieving resides in their power to alter our very way of being. As Emily Dickinson once wrote,

Heavenly Hurt, it gives us—
We can find no scar,
But internal differences,
Where the Meanings, are.

And, as awkward as our progress may have seemed as we mapped our own movement through loss and grief, we created these *internal differences*, these *Meanings*, by our personal choices. In so doing, we have given shape to our here-and-now most precious life.

ELIZABETH HARPER NEELD

Go to **www.elizabethharperneeld.com** to see photographs, read monthly newsletters, find resources for things that help during tough transitions, check out recommendations for books, music, and even recipes, and view other of Elizabeth's books, tapes, and videos. To order *Seven Choices: A Pocket Guide* go to **www.centerpointpress.com**.